Java Programming Easy to Use Guide for Beginners

Understanding the Benefits of Java Syntax

By

Bryden Adriel

Table of Contents

CHAPTER 1
Introduction

1.1 What is Java

Java is a powerful, versatile, and widely-used programming language that has been a mainstay in the software development industry for several decades. Created by James Gosling and his team at Sun Microsystems (now owned by Oracle Corporation), Java was first released in 1995. What sets Java apart from many other programming languages is its platform independence, robustness, and versatility.

Java is often referred to as a "write once, run anywhere" language. This means that you can write Java code on one platform (such as Windows) and run it on another platform (such as macOS or Linux) without modification. This is achieved through the use of the Java Virtual Machine (JVM), which interprets and executes Java bytecode, making it platform-independent. This portability makes Java an ideal choice for developing applications that need to run on a variety of devices and operating systems.

Java is an object-oriented language, which means it encourages a structured approach to programming, focusing on the creation and manipulation of objects. This makes it easier to organize and manage complex codebases and promotes code reusability.

Java has a rich standard library that provides pre-built classes and methods for various tasks, ranging from basic input and output to advanced networking and graphical user interface (GUI) development. This extensive library of classes and packages simplifies the development process and saves developers from reinventing the wheel for common tasks.

In addition to its versatility, Java is also known for its security features. Java applications run inside a secure sandbox environment, which helps prevent malicious code from causing harm to the host system. This makes Java a popular choice for developing web applications, mobile apps, and enterprise-level software where security is paramount.

1.2 Why Learn Java

There are several compelling reasons
to learn Java:

1. **High Demand in the Job
   Market:** Java developers are in
   high demand across various
   industries. Learning Java can open
   up a wide range of job
   opportunities in software
   development, web development,
   mobile app development, and
   more.

2. **Versatility:** Java can be used for a
   wide range of applications,
   including web development,
   mobile app development
   (Android), server-side
   programming, enterprise-level
   software, scientific computing, and
   more. This versatility ensures that

Java developers are always in demand.

3. **Platform Independence:** Java's "write once, run anywhere" philosophy means that the skills you acquire are not tied to a specific operating system or device, making it future-proof and adaptable to changing technology trends.

4. **Robust and Reliable:** Java's strong typing, exception handling, and memory management features contribute to the creation of robust and reliable applications. This is crucial for mission-critical systems.

5. **Community and Resources:** Java has a vast and active developer community, which means you can find extensive resources, tutorials,

and libraries to help you learn and solve problems.

6. **Excellent Learning Path for Beginners:** Java is often recommended as a first programming language for beginners due to its readability, straightforward syntax, and extensive documentation.

7. **Scalability:** Java is known for its ability to handle large-scale projects and applications. This makes it a top choice for developing enterprise-level software.

1.3 Setting Up Your Development Environment

Before you start programming in Java, it's essential to set up your development environment. This typically involves the following steps:

1. **Install the Java Development Kit (JDK):** The JDK includes everything you need to develop Java applications, including the Java compiler (**javac**) and the Java Runtime Environment (JRE). Download and install the appropriate JDK version for your operating system from the official Oracle website or adopt OpenJDK, which is an open-source alternative.

2. **Set Up an Integrated Development Environment**

(IDE): While you can write Java code in a simple text editor, using an IDE can significantly enhance your productivity. Popular Java IDEs include Eclipse, IntelliJ IDEA, and NetBeans. These IDEs provide features like code completion, debugging tools, and project management capabilities.

3. **Configure Your IDE:** After installing the IDE, configure it to use the JDK you installed. Set up code formatting preferences, choose a code style guide, and configure any necessary plugins or extensions for Java development.

4. **Create Your First Java Project:** Once your development environment is set up, create a new Java project or open an existing one. You can then start writing,

compiling, and running Java code within your IDE.

5. **Learn to Use Build Tools:** Familiarize yourself with build tools like Apache Maven or Gradle, which help manage project dependencies and build processes. These tools are commonly used in Java development to streamline the build and deployment of applications.

6. **Explore Documentation and Tutorials:** Java has extensive documentation available online. Take advantage of official Java documentation, online tutorials, and forums to learn more about the language and its features.

7. **Practice, Practice, Practice:** Learning Java, like any programming language, is best

done through hands-on practice. Start with simple programs, gradually tackle more complex projects, and don't be afraid to make mistakes and learn from them.

Java is a powerful and versatile programming language with a rich history and a bright future. Learning Java opens up a world of possibilities in software development, and setting up your development environment is the first step on your journey to becoming a proficient Java developer. Whether you're a beginner or an experienced programmer, Java offers a robust platform for building a wide range of applications.

CHAPTER 2

Getting Started with Java

2.1 Your First Java Program

first steps into the world of Java programming are by creating a simple "Hello, World!" program. This classic introductory program serves as a foundation for understanding the basic structure of a Java program and how to execute it

- **Introduction to the Main Method:** Every Java program starts with a **main** method, which serves as the entry point for your code.

- **Writing and Printing Output:** Learning how to use the **System.out.println()** statement to display text on the console. In this case, you'll print the traditional "Hello, World!" message.

- **Compiling and Running Java Code:** Understanding the process of compiling your Java source code into bytecode using the Java compiler (**javac**) and executing it with the Java Virtual Machine (JVM).

- **Common Pitfalls and Errors:** We'll highlight common mistakes that beginners often make and provide guidance on troubleshooting and fixing errors.

2.2 Understanding Java Syntax

Java, like any programming language, has a specific syntax that you must follow to write correct and meaningful code. We will delve into deeper into Java's syntax, including:

- **Basic Structure of a Java Program:** We will explore how Java programs are organized, including packages, imports, and class definitions.

- **Comments:** Learn how to add comments to your code to provide explanations and documentation for yourself and other developers.

- **Variables and Data Types:** Introduce the concept of variables and how to declare them. We will also discover the various data types in Java, such as integers, floating-point numbers, characters, and strings.

- **Operators:** Understand how to use operators for arithmetic, comparison, and logical operations. These are fundamental for performing calculations and making decisions in your programs.

- **Control Flow:** Get a glimpse into conditional statements (like **if** and **switch**) and loops (such as **for**, **while**, and **do-while**) that control the flow of your program based on certain conditions.

2.3 Variables and Data Types in Java

Variables are essential components of any programming language, including Java. We will dive deeper into variables and data types:

- **Declaring Variables:** Learn how to declare variables in Java, specifying their data type and name. Understand the rules for naming variables.

- **Primitive Data Types:** Explore the various primitive data types in Java, including **int**, **double**, **char**, **boolean**, and more. Understand their ranges and use cases.

- **Initializing Variables:** Discover how to assign values

to variables during declaration or at a later point in your code.

- **Type Casting:** Understand how to convert between different data types, including implicit and explicit type casting.

- **String Data Type:** Explore the **String** class in Java, which represents text and provides various methods for string manipulation.

- **Constants:** Learn about constants and how to declare them using the **final** keyword. Constants are variables whose values cannot be changed once set.

- **Scope of Variables:** Understand variable scope, including local variables,

instance variables, and class
variables (also known as static
variables).

- **Best Practices:** Explore best
practices for naming variables,
choosing appropriate data
types, and optimizing memory
usage.

CHAPTER 3

Control Flow and Decision Making

3.1 Conditional Statements (if, else, switch)

Conditional statements are essential for controlling the flow of a program based on certain conditions. we will explore various conditional constructs in Java:

- **The if Statement:** Learn how to use the **if** statement to execute a block of code if a specified condition is true. Understand the role of boolean expressions in determining whether the code block is executed.

- **The else Statement:** Extend your knowledge to include the **else** statement, which allows you to specify an alternative code block to execute when the condition in the **if** statement is false.

- **The else if Statement:** Explore the use of **else if** statements for handling multiple conditions sequentially.

- **The switch Statement:** Discover the **switch** statement, which provides an elegant way to choose among multiple code blocks based on the value of a variable or expression. Learn about **case** labels and the **default** case.

- **Nested Conditionals:** Understand how to nest **if** statements within other **if** or **else** blocks to handle more complex decision-making scenarios.

- **Ternary Operator (? :):** Introduce the ternary operator as a concise way to express conditional expressions in a single line.

- **Best Practices:** Explore best practices for writing clean and readable conditional statements, including code indentation and style conventions.

3.2 Loops (for, while, do-while)

Loops are used to repeat a block of code multiple times, making them essential for tasks like iterating over arrays, processing data, and implementing repetitive operation, we will delve into the types of loops available in Java:

- **The for Loop:** Learn how to use the **for** loop to execute a block of code repeatedly for a specified number of iterations. Understand the structure of the **for** loop, including initialization, condition, and update expressions.

- **The while Loop:** Explore the **while** loop, which continues to execute a block of code as long as a specified condition remains true. Be aware of the potential for infinite loops and how to avoid them.

- **The do-while Loop:** Understand the **do-while** loop, which is similar to the **while** loop but guarantees that the code block is executed at least once, even if the condition is initially false.

- **Loop Control Statements:** Discover control statements like **break** and **continue** that allow you to modify the flow of loops. Learn how to use them effectively to exit loops prematurely or skip specific iterations.

- **Nested Loops:** Explore the concept of nested loops, where one loop is contained within another. Understand how to use nested loops for tasks that require multiple levels of iteration.

- **Enhanced for Loop (for-each):** Introduce the enhanced **for** loop, also known as the for-each loop, which simplifies iteration over arrays and collections.

- **Best Practices:** Learn best practices for loop design, including choosing the appropriate loop type, optimizing loop performance, and maintaining code readability.

3.3 Handling User Input

Interacting with users and collecting input is a crucial aspect of many Java applications. We will learn how to handle user input effectively:

- **Using Scanner for Input:** Understand how to use the **Scanner** class to read input from the keyboard. Learn how to create **Scanner** objects and read various data types such as integers, floating-point numbers, strings, and characters.

- **Input Validation:** Explore techniques for validating user input to ensure it meets the expected criteria, such as checking for valid numeric input or preventing input errors.

- **Handling Exceptions:** Learn how to handle exceptions that may occur when reading user input, such as input mismatch exceptions, and use try-catch blocks to gracefully manage these situations.

- **Menu-Driven Programs:** Discover how to create menu-driven programs where users can select options from a menu and perform different actions based on their choices.

- **Interactive Programs:** Learn to design interactive programs that continuously prompt the user for input until a specific condition is met, such as entering "quit" to exit the program.

- **Best Practices:** Explore best practices for providing clear and user-friendly input prompts and error messages to enhance the user experience.

CHAPTER 4

Java Functions and Methods

4.1 Creating and Calling Functions

Functions (also known as methods in Java) are blocks of reusable code that perform specific tasks.

- **Method Declaration:** Understand the syntax for declaring methods in Java. Learn about method names, return types, and access modifiers (public, private, protected, etc.).

- **Method Body:** Explore the block of code within a method that defines its functionality. This is where you write the instructions for what the method should do.

- **Method Signature:** Learn about the method signature, which includes the method name and its parameter list. Understand how method overloading allows you to define multiple methods with the same name but different parameter lists.

- **Calling Methods:** Discover how to call methods from other parts of your program. Learn about invoking methods and passing arguments.

- **Void Methods:** Understand methods that do not return a

value (void methods) and their use cases.

- **Static Methods:** Introduce static methods, which belong to the class rather than an instance of the class. Learn how to call static methods and when to use them.

4.2 Parameters and Return Values

Parameters and return values are essential components of Java methods, allowing you to pass data into a method and receive results back. We will explore these concepts in detail:

- **Method Parameters:** Learn how to define parameters in a method's parameter list.

Understand the difference
between formal parameters (in
the method declaration) and
actual arguments (passed when
calling the method).

- **Passing Arguments:** Explore
  different ways to pass
  arguments to methods,
  including by value and by
  reference (for objects).
  Understand how method
  parameters work with primitive
  data types and objects.

- **Return Values:** Understand
  how to specify a return type for
  a method. Learn how to use the
  return statement to send a
  value back to the calling code.

- **Returning Multiple Values:**
  Discover techniques for
  returning multiple values from

a method, such as using arrays, objects, or custom data structures.

- **Method Overloading:** Revisit method overloading, focusing on how it allows you to define methods with the same name but different parameter lists. Learn how the Java compiler determines which method to call based on the arguments provided.

4.3 Scope and Lifetime of Variables

The scope and lifetime of variables determine where a variable is accessible and how long it exists. We will explore these concepts and their implications:

- **Variable Scope:** Understand the scope of variables, which defines where in your code a variable can be accessed. Learn about local variables (limited to a specific block or method), instance variables (belonging to an object), and class variables (shared among all instances of a class).

- **Variable Lifetime:** Explore how the lifetime of a variable corresponds to its existence in memory. Learn how local variables have a shorter lifetime than instance or class variables.

- **Variable Shadowing:** Understand variable shadowing, where a variable in a nested scope has the same name as a variable in an outer scope. Learn how to distinguish between shadowed variables.

- **Method Parameters and Scope:** Discover how method parameters have local scope within the method and may shadow other variables with the same name in outer scopes.

- **Garbage Collection:** Learn how the Java Virtual Machine (JVM) automatically manages memory and deallocates objects when they are no longer in use through a process called garbage collection.

- **Best Practices:** Explore best practices for variable naming, scope management, and minimizing the use of global variables, which can lead to

code that is harder to maintain
and debug.

CHAPTER 5

Object-Oriented Programming (OOP) in Java

5.1 Introduction to OOP

Object-Oriented Programming (OOP) is a programming paradigm that revolves around the concept of objects.

- **Object-Oriented Concepts:** Explore the fundamental concepts of OOP, including objects, classes, inheritance, encapsulation, and polymorphism.

- **Advantages of OOP:**
Understand the benefits of
OOP, such as code reusability,
modularity, and ease of
maintenance.

- **Objects in the Real World:**
Relate OOP concepts to real-
world objects and scenarios to
gain a practical understanding
of how OOP mirrors the real
world.

- **OOP Principles:** Learn about
key OOP principles, such as
abstraction, encapsulation,
inheritance, and polymorphism,
and how they apply in Java.

5.2 Classes and Objects

In Java, classes and objects are the
building blocks of OOP. We will

delve into the creation and usage of classes and objects:

- **Class Definition:** Understand how to define a class in Java, including defining fields (attributes) and methods (functions).

- **Object Creation:** Learn how to create objects from a class. Explore the use of the **new** keyword and the constructor method.

- **Instance Variables:** Explore instance variables (also known as member variables or attributes), which hold the state of an object.

- **Methods:** Understand how methods define the behavior of objects. Learn how to call methods on objects.

- **Constructors:** Discover the role of constructors in initializing objects. Explore parameterized constructors and default constructors.

- **Static Members:** Introduce static variables and methods, which are associated with the class itself rather than instances of the class.

5.3 Inheritance and Polymorphism

Inheritance and polymorphism are powerful OOP concepts that allow you to create hierarchical and flexible code structures.

- **Inheritance:** Learn how to create subclasses (derived classes) that inherit attributes and behaviors from a superclass (base class). Understand the **extends** keyword and the **super** keyword for invoking superclass constructors and methods.

- **Types of Inheritance:** Explore different types of inheritance, including single inheritance (a subclass inherits from one superclass) and multiple inheritance (a subclass inherits from multiple superclasses through interfaces).

- **Polymorphism:** Understand polymorphism as the ability of objects to take on multiple forms. Learn how method overriding allows a subclass to provide its own implementation of a method inherited from a superclass.

- **Method Overloading:** Revisit method overloading and its role in polymorphism. Understand how it allows you to define multiple methods with the same name but different parameters within the same class.

- **Interfaces:** Discover interfaces as a way to define contracts for classes. Learn how to implement interfaces in Java classes and how they enable polymorphism.

- **Abstract Classes:** Introduce abstract classes, which cannot be instantiated directly but serve as templates for concrete subclasses. Understand the **abstract** keyword and abstract methods.

- **Casting and Type Compatibility:** Explore casting in Java, including upcasting (implicit casting) and downcasting (explicit casting). Learn how to check the type of an object using the **instanceof** operator.

- **Dynamic Binding:** Understand dynamic method binding, which allows the JVM to determine the appropriate method implementation to call at runtime based on the actual object type.

CHAPTER 6

Working with Data in Java

6.1 Arrays and Lists

Arrays and lists are fundamental data structures in Java that allow you to store and manipulate collections of data efficiently. We will explore how to work with arrays and lists:

- **Arrays:** Understand how to declare, initialize, and manipulate arrays in Java. Explore single-dimensional and multi-dimensional arrays, including arrays of primitive types and objects.

- **ArrayList:** Learn about the **ArrayList** class from the Java Collections Framework, which provides dynamic resizing and more flexible operations compared to traditional arrays.

- **Array vs. ArrayList:** Compare the advantages and disadvantages of arrays and **ArrayLists** in different scenarios. Understand when to choose one over the other.

- **Common Array and ArrayList Operations:** Explore common operations such as adding and removing elements, accessing elements by index, iterating through elements, and sorting arrays or lists.

- **Iterating through Arrays and Lists:** Discover different methods for iterating through arrays and

ArrayLists, including traditional loops, enhanced **for** loops, and using iterators.

- **Searching and Sorting:** Learn how to perform searching and sorting operations on arrays and lists, including linear and binary search algorithms and sorting algorithms like bubble sort and quicksort.

6.2 Working with Strings

Strings are essential for working with text data in Java. We will delve into string manipulation and processing:

- **String Basics:** Understand how to declare and initialize strings in Java. Learn about string concatenation, common string operations, and the use of escape sequences.

- **String Methods:** Explore the methods available in the **String** class for tasks such as substring extraction, string comparison, case conversion, and more.

- **String Manipulation:** Learn how to manipulate strings by splitting, joining, and replacing substrings. Understand how to format strings using placeholders.

- **Regular Expressions:** Introduce regular expressions (regex) and their role in pattern matching and text manipulation. Learn how to use the **Pattern** and **Matcher** classes for regex operations.

- **StringBuilder and StringBuffer:** Discover the **StringBuilder** and **StringBuffer** classes for efficient

string concatenation and
modification, especially in
scenarios involving large amounts
of string manipulation.

6.3 File Input and Output

Working with files allows your Java
programs to read and write data to
external storage. We will explore file
input and output operations:

- **File Handling Basics:** Understand
  how to work with files in Java,
  including creating, opening,
  closing, reading, and writing files.

- **File Streams:** Learn about input
  and output streams for reading
  from and writing to files. Explore
  classes like **FileInputStream**,
  FileOutputStream, **FileReader**,
  and **FileWriter**.

- **Buffered Streams:** Discover the benefits of using buffered streams (e.g., **BufferedReader** and **BufferedWriter**) to improve file I/O performance.

- **File Paths and Directories:** Understand how to work with file paths, directories, and folder structures. Learn about Java's **File** class for file and directory manipulation.

- **Exception Handling:** Explore error handling and exception handling techniques when dealing with file I/O, including handling **IOExceptions**.

- **Reading and Writing Text and Binary Files:** Learn how to read and write both text and binary files in Java. Understand the differences between these two approaches.

- **Serialization:** Introduce object serialization and deserialization, which allows you to save and restore objects to and from files.

CHAPTER 7
Exception Handling

7.1 Understanding Exceptions

Exception handling is a crucial aspect of Java programming, allowing you to gracefully handle errors and unexpected situations.

- **What are Exceptions:** Understand what exceptions are and why they are essential in Java. An exception is an abnormal condition or error that occurs during the execution of a program.

- **Types of Exceptions:** Explore the hierarchy of exceptions in Java, including checked exceptions (e.g.,

IOException) and unchecked exceptions (e.g., **NullPointerException**).

- **Exception Classes:** Learn about the base class for exceptions in Java, **java.lang.Throwable**, and its subclasses **java.lang.Exception** and **java.lang.RuntimeException**.

- **Checked vs. Unchecked Exceptions:** Understand the difference between checked exceptions, which must be handled or declared in the method signature, and unchecked exceptions, which do not require explicit handling.

- **Exception Stack Trace:** Explore the concept of a stack trace, which provides information about the sequence of method calls that led to an exception.

7.2 Handling Exceptions

We will delve into how to handle exceptions effectively to prevent program crashes and provide meaningful error messages:

- **Try-Catch Blocks:** Understand the **try-catch** mechanism, which allows you to catch exceptions and handle them gracefully. Learn how to specify the code to be monitored in the **try** block and the corresponding error-handling code in the **catch** block.

- **Multiple Catch Blocks:** Discover how to use multiple **catch** blocks to handle different types of exceptions. Catch blocks are evaluated in order, and the first matching block is executed.

- **The finally Block:** Introduce the **finally** block, which is used to define code that must be executed, whether an exception occurs or not. This is often used for cleanup tasks, such as closing files or network connections.

- **Throwing Exceptions:** Learn how to use the **throw** statement to explicitly throw exceptions when specific conditions are met. This allows you to create custom error messages and handle exceptional cases.

- **Exception Propagation:** Understand how exceptions propagate up the call stack if they are not caught and handled at the current level. Learn about the role of checked and unchecked exceptions in this process.

- **Checked Exceptions in Method Signatures:** Explore how to declare checked exceptions in method signatures using the **throws** keyword. This informs callers that the method may throw specific exceptions that need to be handled.

- **Handling Unchecked Exceptions:** Learn about best practices for handling unchecked exceptions, which are often related to programming errors. Understand how to prevent them and improve program robustness.

7.3 Custom Exceptions

While Java provides a wide range of built-in exception classes, you can also create your custom exceptions to handle application-specific errors:

- **Creating Custom Exceptions:**
  Understand how to create custom
  exception classes by extending the
  Exception or **RuntimeException**
  classes. Define constructors and
  error messages for your custom
  exceptions.

- **Throwing Custom Exceptions:**
  Learn how to throw custom
  exceptions when your code
  encounters specific error
  conditions that are not adequately
  represented by built-in exceptions.

- **Handling Custom Exceptions:**
  Discover how to catch and handle
  custom exceptions using **try-catch**
  blocks, just like built-in
  exceptions. Custom exceptions
  allow you to add context-specific
  information to error messages.

- **Best Practices:** Explore best practices for designing and using custom exceptions effectively, including naming conventions and when to use custom exceptions versus built-in ones.

CHAPTER 8

Introduction to Java Libraries

8.1 Using Built-in Java Libraries

Java comes with a rich standard library that provides a wide range of pre-built classes and methods for various tasks. We will explore how to leverage these built-in libraries:

- **java.lang Package:** Learn about the core **java.lang** package, which provides fundamental classes like **Object**, **String**, and **Exception**. Understand how these classes are automatically imported and available in every Java program.

- **java.util Package:** Explore the **java.util** package, which includes classes for data structures like lists, sets, maps, and arrays. Learn about classes such as **ArrayList**, **HashMap**, and **Date** for common programming tasks.

- **Input and Output (I/O):** Understand how to use classes from the **java.io** package for reading from and writing to files, as well as classes from the **java.nio** package for more advanced I/O operations.

- **java.net Package:** Learn about the **java.net** package, which provides classes for networking, including client and server communication using sockets and URLs.

- **Concurrency and Multithreading:** Explore the

java.util.concurrent package, which offers classes for managing threads, synchronization, and concurrent data structures.

- **Date and Time:** Discover the **java.time** package, introduced in Java 8, for handling date and time operations. Learn about classes like **LocalDate**, **LocalTime**, and **DateTimeFormatter**.

- **Utility Classes:** Explore other utility classes in the standard library, such as **Math** for mathematical operations, **Arrays** for array manipulation, and **Collections** for working with collections.

8.2 Third-Party Libraries and APIs

While Java's standard library is extensive, there are situations where you may need additional functionality provided by third-party libraries and APIs:

- **Maven and Gradle:** Learn about build automation tools like Maven and Gradle, which simplify the management of project dependencies and the inclusion of third-party libraries.

- **Popular Java Libraries:** Explore some of the most commonly used third-party libraries and APIs in the Java ecosystem, such as Apache Commons, Google Guava, Jackson for JSON processing, and Hibernate for database access.

- **Adding External Libraries:** Understand how to add external libraries to your Java project by including them in your build configuration (e.g., **pom.xml** for Maven or **build.gradle** for Gradle).

- **API Documentation:** Learn how to access and navigate the documentation for third-party libraries to understand their usage and capabilities.

- **Customizing Dependencies:** Discover how to customize the versions and configurations of third-party dependencies to suit your project's requirements.

8.3 GUI Programming with Swing

Graphical User Interfaces (GUIs) are essential for building interactive desktop applications. We will explore GUI programming in Java using the Swing library:

- **Introduction to Swing:** Understand what Swing is and how it fits into Java's GUI development ecosystem.

- **Swing Components:** Explore Swing's rich set of components, including buttons, labels, text fields, combo boxes, and more. Learn how to create and customize these components to build user-friendly interfaces.

- **Layout Management:** Discover layout managers in Swing, such as

FlowLayout, **BorderLayout**, and **GridLayout**, for controlling the arrangement of components within a GUI.

- **Event Handling:** Learn how to handle user interactions and events (e.g., button clicks, mouse actions) in Swing applications by registering event listeners and defining event-handling code.

- **Dialogs and Windows:** Understand how to create dialog boxes, message boxes, and separate windows in Swing applications.

- **Swing Application Structure:** Explore the typical structure of a Swing application, including creating the main frame, adding components, and defining event handlers.

- **Look and Feel:** Learn about Swing's "look and feel" feature, which allows you to customize the appearance of your GUI to match the platform on which it runs.

CHAPTER 9

Debugging and Testing

9.1 Common Debugging Techniques

Debugging is the process of identifying and fixing errors (bugs) in your code. We will delve into common debugging techniques in Java:

- **Print Statements:** Understand how to use **System.out.println()** statements to print variable values, messages, and debugging information to the console.

- **Debugger:** Learn how to use integrated development

environments (IDEs) like Eclipse, IntelliJ IDEA, or Visual Studio Code to set breakpoints, step through code, inspect variables, and analyze program execution.

- **Logging:** Explore Java's logging framework, such as the **java.util.logging** package, to create log files and record application events for debugging and monitoring.

- **Exception Handling:** Review exception handling techniques to catch and handle runtime exceptions gracefully, including logging error details.

- **Unit Testing:** Introduce the concept of unit testing, which involves writing small, focused tests for individual units (such as methods or classes) of your code.

9.2 Writing Unit Tests

Unit testing is an essential practice for ensuring the correctness of your code.

- **JUnit Framework:** Explore the JUnit framework, a popular Java library for writing and running unit tests. Learn how to set up JUnit in your project.

- **Test Cases:** Create test cases and test methods using JUnit's annotations, such as **@Test**, to define test scenarios and assertions.

- **Assert Statements:** Understand how to use JUnit's assert statements, such as **assertEquals**, **assertTrue**, and **assertFalse**, to verify expected outcomes in your tests.

- **Test Fixtures:** Discover how to set up and tear down test fixtures using **@Before** and **@After** annotations, ensuring a consistent test environment.

- **Test Suites:** Learn how to organize multiple test cases into test suites using the **@RunWith** and **@Suite** annotations.

- **Mocking:** Introduce the concept of mocking frameworks like Mockito for creating mock objects to simulate behavior and interactions in unit tests.

9.3 Debugging Tools

- **Integrated Development Environments (IDEs):** Understand how IDEs like Eclipse, IntelliJ IDEA, and NetBeans provide powerful debugging features, including breakpoints, watchlists, variable inspection, and step-by-step execution.

- **Command-Line Debugging:** Learn about command-line debugging tools like **jdb** (Java Debugger) for debugging Java applications outside of an IDE.

- **Logging Frameworks:** Explore Java logging frameworks such as **java.util.logging**, Log4j, and Logback for recording application events, errors, and debug information.

- **Profiling Tools:** Discover profiling tools like VisualVM and YourKit for analyzing the performance of your Java applications and identifying bottlenecks.

- **Static Analysis Tools:** Learn about static code analysis tools like FindBugs, PMD, and Checkstyle for identifying code quality issues, potential bugs, and style violations.

- **Code Coverage Tools:** Understand how code coverage tools like JaCoCo and Cobertura help measure the percentage of code executed by your tests, ensuring comprehensive coverage.